All Diaspora's Children

All Diaspora's Children

Poems by

Johanna DeMay

© 2025 Johanna DeMay. All rights reserved.
This material may not be reproduced in any form, published,
reprinted, recorded, performed, broadcast,
rewritten, or redistributed without
the explicit permission of Johanna DeMay.
All such actions are strictly prohibited by law.

Cover design by Shay Culligan
Cover image by Fang Xia Nuo
Author photo by Will DeMay

ISBN: 978-1-63980-719-2

Kelsay Books
502 South 1040 East, A-119
American Fork, Utah 84003
Kelsaybooks.com

to Will, and to our children, born and chosen:

Rafael
Alexandra
Michael
Laura

Acknowledgments

With deep gratitude to the publications where these poems first appeared or are forthcoming, some in earlier versions or with different titles:

Big Windows Review: "Reasonable Doubt"
Burningword Literary Journal: "Shrinking"
Concho River Review: "Needlework"
Constellations—A Journal of Poetry and Fiction: "How We Were Raised," "Marcela's Quest," "Haunted"
From Everywhere a Little—a Migration Anthology: "All Diaspora's Children"
The Healing Muse: "Remission Is a Dormant Volcano"
I-70 Review: "Blind Spots," "Human Remains"
Loch Raven Review: "What Our Bones Believe," "If English Nouns Had Gender," "Ghost Town," "Marcela's Lament," "At Night," "The Food Chain," "Cave People"
The MacGuffin: "My Husband's Pacemaker"
The Ocotillo Review: "Pueblo Bonito's Ghosts"
Rust & Moth: "Memory Is a Telescope"
Thimble Literary Magazine: "Starting from Scratch"

Personal acknowledgments:

No book reaches a reader's hands without the dedicated work of many other hands. I am grateful to the editors and staff of Kelsay Books for bringing this book into your hands.

I am grateful to family and friends, teachers and mentors both living and dead. The following are some of those early teachers and mentors, blessed memories all:

Thank you, Mrs. Rose Shanoff, second grade teacher. You saw something in the tongue-tied child seated in the last row pretending to be invisible. You kept me after school and read to me.

Thank you, Mrs. Ethel Figueroa, Elementary school librarian at the American School in Mexico City. You made a refuge for me; you led me to books about young girls and wild places.

Thank you, Mr. Gilbert Weatherbee, my English and Creative Writing teacher through four years of high school. Because you believed in me, you pushed me hard, always demanding more of me. I will never stop pushing.

Thank you, black-listed poet George Oppen, and screen writer Albert Maltz, fellow expatriates. You read my teenage scribblings and said, "Yes Johanna, you can be a writer."

Inspired poets, teachers and mentors, (most) still living:

Thank you, Jennifer Cement, Director of the San Miguel Poetry Week, and invited faculty, especially Carol Ann Duffy, Thomas Lux, Kevin Young, Therese Svoboda, and Tony Barnstone.

Thank you, Marge Piercy, and the poets you gathered for your Poetry Intensive Workshop in 2022. We are grateful for your lifetime of passionate commitment—to writing, to poetry, to your students, and to causes that matter.

Thank you, Piercy Group poets, especially Deborah Leipziger, Mary K. O'Melvany, Jessica Simon and Steven Stark, for continuing support and insightful feedback.

Editors, colleagues, friends and family members:

Thank you, Editors who have published my work, especially those who have given space to my poems about immigrants in my community. Thank you, Hilda Raz, editor of *bosque* and ABQ inPrint. Thank you, Dan Cuddy, editor of Loch Raven Review, and Nadia Arioli, editor of Thimble Literary Magazine. Thank you, Nina Rubinstein Alonso, editor of Constellations, a Literary Magazine of Poetry and Prose. You have shared this journey.

Thank you, Diana Anhalt, poet, historian of the Black-listed community in Mexico City, peerless teacher, life-long friend whom I first met in our high school creative writing class. Without you, my poems would probably have remained buried in cardboard file boxes.

Thank you, Susan D'Lamater, thoughtful reader, indispensable friend. Your comments make my poems better. During long conversations on our walks in the Bosque and at neighborhood café tables, you make our blue skies shine a brighter blue.

Thank you, Professor A. Charlene McDermott, for over fifty years of friendship and numberless books you have given me—your friendship enriches my life, your books have enriched my mind.

Thank you, friends and fellow volunteers at Plaza de Encuentro, a non-profit organization serving the immigrant community, for the work you do, and for welcoming me onto the team.

Thank you members of the immigrant community, for the wealth of experience, wisdom and warmth you bring, for the work you do to protect your families and support your *compañeros,* and for welcoming me into the community.

Thank you, Will, my soul's partner. Your belief in me gives me courage to aim high, you are my bedrock and my wings, you make possible everything I do.

Contents

Part 1: Ties of Blood and Bone

All Diaspora's Children	19
In the Comfort Zone of Her Own Black Skin	20
About Change	21
Marcela's Quest	23
Haunted	24
The Grandson Tree	26
Lifelines	27
Remission Is a Dormant Volcano	28
My Grandson Announces He's Engaged	29
Buried Secrets	31
Memory Is a Telescope	32

Part 2: What Our Bones Believe

What Our Bones Believe	37
Reasonable Doubt	39
Earthen Vessels	40
Paul Robeson Teaches Me to Fly	42
A Heart Is Not a Valentine	43
Proof Positive	44
Invasive Species	45
If English Nouns Had Gender	47
My Husband's Pacemaker	49
Pueblo Bonito's Ghosts	51
20 Pages, 100 Questions	52

Part 3: Stress Fractures

How We Were Raised	57
Grace's Broken Statue	59
The Performer	61

Needlework	62
Nuclear Triptych	64
Ghost Town	68
Starting from Scratch	70
The Language Barrier	72
Blind Spots	74
Routine Screening	76
Shrinking	78
While Fractures and Abrasions Heal	80
Epitaph	81

Part 4: Knit Together

Wheelchair-Guy at the Sidewalk Cafe	85
Among Kin	87
Showing Up	88
Knit Together	89
State Road #57	90
Human Remains	92
What Our Bodies Know	94
A Visitation	96
Old People	98
The Food Chain	99
Elegy for Our Garden	101
Cave People	102
Concerto	104

Caminante, no hay camino . . .
se hace el camino al andar.

   —Proverbios y cantares (XXIX)
    by Antonio Machado

Traveler, there is no road.
We make the road as we go.

   —Translation by Johanna DeMay

Part 1:
Ties of Blood and Bone

All Diaspora's Children

My looks convey no subliminal threat.
The Midwestern English I learned at my mother's breast
betrays no trace of my other languages.

But my heart's drenched in bougainvillea's purple,
cempasúchil's orange and yellow—colors
of the country where I grew up.

Wary of racial profiling, my son carries documentation.
His Asian wife deflects crass remarks in her native tongue
—Minnesota's Swedish-inflected sing-song lilt.

They've trained my ears to register
background buzz of racial tropes.
Browsing my neighborhood bookstore

I'm hooked by a title, find the poet's head shot.
Young Palestinian-American, she threads Arabic script
through English text—filigree pinned to plain cotton.

Writes of her father murdered in Gaza,
uncle tortured in prison, mother gutted by grief.
Lessons learned growing up in exile:

how to breathe through lung-busting terror
each New Year's Eve, every Fourth of July;
how to glide like a queen in her blue silk hijab

past hostile glares, hurtful words—
without lowering her gaze,
without lengthening her stride.

We are all diaspora's children.
I buy the poet's book.

In the Comfort Zone of Her Own Black Skin

One blustery November night when my neighbor Marie
was recovering from surgery, I made her cream of mushroom

soup with puff-balls and porcinis we'd gathered in the Jemez
mountains. In the comfort zone of her narrow bedroom,

wrapped up in quilts and candlelight, we cradled our bowls
in chilled hands, savored the gifts of last summer's monsoon

while winter's angry gusts clawed at her windows.
Her roommate breezed in—bangles, shawls, long red skirt,

silver nail polish like sparklers on the 4th of July.
A medical resident on the cusp, Aisha had seen everything.

She had stories to tell. Awestruck, I wanted to hear them all.
How could she do the unthinkable?

It's not that hard. You could do it too.
See children suffer? Watch people die?

Carve up a human body as if it were a side of beef?
What do you feel when you cut them, in the morgue?

She shrugged. *It's just a job—never bothered me—until my first
black body. Then I ran into the hallway and puked.*

She chuckled, at ease
in the comfort zone of her own black skin.

About Change

In a world where only the seasons changed,
my father fled his burning *shtetl.* Change meant

escape from blood-crazed Cossacks; sub-zero nights
in drafty cabins, studying Torah by candlelight.

Whippings for writing left-handed,
for liking Romani girls better than books.

In Odessa he boarded a freighter, shouldered cargo,
shoveled coal, sluiced latrines, polished officers' boots.

Did he shout when he spotted Lady Liberty's torch?
Broadway's constellation of tethered stars?

On the Lower East Side he found kinfolk,
shrugged when *goyim* said he didn't belong.

He outlived horse-drawn carriages, coal powered steamships,
watched Neil Armstrong bounce on the pockmarked moon.

Fourth-generation Americans, my grandsons explore continents,
oceans, galaxies on their laptop computers, train for careers

that don't yet exist. Students at their high school
speak eighteen different languages at home.

In old Jewish neighborhoods, new Americans speak Spanish,
Arabic, Farsi, Vietnamese—own restaurants that serve

exotic spicy foods. *Mariachi* music and *cumbias*
drive klezmer bands and polkas from the airwaves.

What would my father tell his great-grandsons about change?
What would they tell my father about who belongs?

Marcela's Quest

Despite our shared language, Marcela insists
I don't understand. She tells me again:
> *I never intended to leave Honduras.*
>
> *Esteban, my youngest—now Estrella—beaten, raped,*
> *bullet in her right leg. Los mareros swore they'd kill her*
> *unless she sold drugs, guns, sex.*
>
> *I dug up the cash her father buried*
> *before MS-13 thugs murdered him.*
> *Put my daughter on a northbound bus.*

Estrella made it to Ciudad Juárez, paid a *coyote,*
crossed the river with six *compañeras,* requested asylum.
La Migra locked them in a private transgenders' jail.

> *Two years ago Estrella stopped calling*
> *but I'm convinced m'hija's alive. Perhaps in LA—*
> *she named herself Estrella—born to be a star.*

I place Esteban's student ID in his mother's hands.
> *Ten million people in LA . . . eight hundred miles away . . .*
> *It's dangerous, Marcela!*

She pockets the card, pulls her rosary from a drawer.
> *4,000 kilometers from Tegucigalpa to El Paso—*
> *five pairs of shoes—jungles, mountains, deserts.*
>
> *I dodged pimps, pushers, gangbangers, traffickers,*
> *cops on the take. God wants me to find her,*
> *sends help when I need it most. He sent you.*

Haunted

Mother was too young to ask where Bubbe Miriam
        came from—Poland? Russia? Ukraine?

Haunted by nightmares, Bubbe spoke little.
        Her precious gold locket? Empty—no faded portrait,

lock of hair, name engraved in Hebrew or Cyrillic.
        Bubbe Miriam died, Mother went to school—

learned English, learned to fend for herself.
        But Mother had nightmares—haunted.

Insomniac child, wary as a stray cat,
        I overheard, *Famine . . . Fire . . . Pogrom . . .*

In Vitepsk—market town near my father's *shtetl*—
        Chagall painted indigo skies, goats playing fiddles, horses,

doves, flying brides. Did Father dream in bright colors?
        When he was fourteen, Cossacks torched barns,

tore down doors, beat mothers, shot fathers,
        raped sisters. Was he haunted?

A century later, on TV news I watch
        Russian tanks invade Ukraine, bomb cities,

flatten schools, hospitals, apartment blocks.
        Yesterday's footage, or a 1940s newsreel?

Even in color, smoldering ruins look much alike.
        Women lead children into exile,

leaving husbands, frail parents, behind.
        Uprooted, transplanted far from home,

how many children will grow up haunted
        —cringe when a car backfires,

lash out when a spouse disagrees—
        throw the first punch—pick up a gun.

The Grandson Tree

(for ISD)

In the twentieth century's final decade, we plant
a cottonwood sapling to celebrate your birth,
confident it will outlast us. It grows,

shades our house, shelters goldfinches, sparrows,
hummingbirds when frenzied wings give out.
Robins awake in the witching hours, like me.

No longer haunted by my parents' nightmares—
poverty, war, genocide—I celebrate the new millennium.
After tempests, could history's arc bring rainbows?

9/11—forever wars in Afghanistan, Iraq; countless massacres
at home—concerts, supermarkets, elementary schools—
the 2016 election. History's arc? Yesterday's rainbow.

In your hometown, Capitol of Minnesota Nice, a teenager
videos George Floyd—handcuffed face-down, neck crushed
beneath a blue-clad knee—while bystanders plead with police.

Your father beats cancer, but the Grandson Tree sickens.
Days before you turn twenty-six, your grandfather
cuts the dead cottonwood down.

When I wish you Happy Birthday, your voice falters.
I remind you, *We belong to the tribe that never quits.*
Your father's still alive.

I don't mention the tree.

Lifelines

No visits while Covid-19 holds us hostage,
but we still talk. Tonight we have a clear signal.

Josefina's voice shakes. Arthritic fingers fumble
her phone. I redial, tell her to take deep breaths.

Last Friday after dialysis Juan colapsed—
no pulse, not breathing. EMTs shocked him,

strapped his limp body onto a gurney,
hoisted him into the ambulance.

Los paramédicos me gritaron en inglés.
Sirens screamed. They took him away.

Legally blind, no family nearby, Josefina prayed to her namesake,
San José—patron saint of immigrants and exiles.

In the ICU a Spanish-speaking nurse named Gloria
called to explain: *Juan's intubated. Condition? Grave . . .*

All night Josefina prayed. This morning, ¡*Un milagro!*
He's breathing on his own! Promised he'll come home soon.

Josefina croons, ¡*San José siempre me escucha!*
Saint Joseph never lets her down.

I praise her courage, ask her to call the minute she hears news.
Cellphones—lifelines on sleepless nights.

Remission Is a Dormant Volcano

My son's in remission.
He's healthy now—no more chemo,
radiation. No blood tests, urine tests,

CAT scans, ultrasounds.
He's in remission.
He's on solid ground.

Remission's a dormant volcano.
Lately he's felt short of breath
—scars on his heart, his lungs.

Average lifespan of long-term survivors?
Ten years less. Volcanoes provide
no solid ground.

Free-climbers scaling a vertical wall,
patients and families cling
to nubbins of crumbly rock,

find toeholds on inch-wide ledges,
face forward, don't look down.
Even atheists bargain with god.

My Grandson Announces He's Engaged

He's just twenty-one, aglow with the same giddy joy I felt
when I first cupped his father's head in my palm,
cradled his tiny body in the crook of my arm.

Fast forward twenty years: my son announces he's in love.
Fast forward again: my son & my grandson—one's coming in
for a landing, the other's revving up for takeoff.

Features forged in the same genetic fire:
dark hair, high foreheads, eye-color stolen
from storm-lashed oceans, dimples.

Matching grins anchored by the same crooked canine.
Only I know the origin of that oddity. Its author
lurks in cobweb-filled corners of dreams—

hall of mirrors where warped memories play
hide & seek. I delete the ghost, mute its smug voice.
Its growling bass notes reverberate in my boys.

My son's gaze wanders, face a creased map
of unforeseen detours—early marriage, parenthood,
divorce. Stymied career, cancer.

I tell my grandson to study his father's face—
reflection of the grown man he'll become.
Like non-refundable one-way tickets,

some decisions can't be undone; last-minute
changes of destination, delays, cancellations
may carry steep costs.

My son cuts in: *Wisdom gained from experience can't be transferred.*
. . . As if I didn't know.

Buried Secrets

Only child of an only child,
through marriage I gain
sixteen aunts and uncles,

twenty-seven cousins,
a front-row seat at the rituals
of a foreign culture.

During a family funeral I overhear
chatty cousins two pews back.
. . . looks like Aunt Emma . . . Jewish.

Did they never wonder why
their Grandma Ruth stayed at home,
tended the stove, skimmed yellow fat

from bubbling chicken broth,
baked apple pies while they attended
Mass at St. Bernadette's?

During sermons, beside freshly dug graves,
tight-lipped composure breaks down,
tears overflow, secrets long-buried resurface.

Memory Is a Telescope

On Facebook my sister-in-law discovers
a photograph of the house

where she and my husband grew up.
Towering sycamores dwarf the roofline.

He recalls he dug the holes deep, tamped down
rich loam. She doesn't remember planting trees.

Memory is a telescope—it gathers light from dead stars,
pinpoints the timeworn farmhouse ten miles from town

—no neighbors, no fences. As gray as loneliness,
sagging curtains shroud narrow windows.

Focus reset, the telescope magnifies dust-motes
adrift in my husband's sweltering attic bedroom—

miniature galaxies spin through twin beams from windows
close-set like roosters' eyes. Under the peaked roof we sleep

among relics: Father's accordion—fire-engine red, keys yellow
like the old man's teeth. Mother's treadle sewing machine,

her mother's buxom Victorian mannequin.
In a cardboard box of dog-eared snapshots

ancestors beg to be named.
The telescope zooms in on edgy face-offs

like freeze-frames in a black & white movie.
In one shoebox bedroom sisters butt heads;

in the other, Father harangues Mother.
The house hisses—a kettle about to boil over.

Muggy days, mind-numbing as after-school detentions,
sweaty nights, dank sheets, mosquitoes' whine . . .

At the vanishing point where our telescopes lose resolution
my husband's memories converge with mine.

Part 2:
What Our Bones Believe

What Our Bones Believe

Strangers ask my Asian daughter-in-law,
my brown skinned son, *What are you?*

Self-appointed census-takers, they require
a label. No one's immune—in kindergarten

I asked a playmate, *Are you Jewish,
or are you Christmas?*

Today, if you ask where I was born,
I deflect the question. Like vote-counts

in gerrymandered districts, some facts
can be misleading. Ask, instead,

where I feel at home, who I care about,
what makes my hackles rise?

What life history has made me the person
I've become? Not how I've made my living,

what my birth certificate says, which box
I ticked on the census form.

My identity's not tribal—it sings in two languages,
sways to cumbia's tropical beat,

craves *totopos con salsa cruda,*
ripe mangos speared on a fork

with a tine like a narwhal's tusk—
juices dripping down knuckles and chin.

Identity's rooted in what our bodies
know, what our bones believe.

Reasonable Doubt

I don't trust Big Pharma, Margaret frets,
but Mexican folk remedies? Mushrooms?

Herbal teas, lime juice, turpentine?
Aren't curanderos just faith healers?

Tepotzlán's ancient shaman, Don Pedro,
blended Náhuatl with Spanish—duet

of reed flute and Flamenco guitar. He patched
my bloody finger with warm belly fat

from a *tlacuache*—Mexico's beloved marsupial.
Tore a strip from my yellow silk scarf

to wrap his handiwork, warned me
not to wash my hand. I had nightmares—

infection, amputation—yet my wounded hand
felt cool, no longer throbbed.

A week later he removed the bandage—
no lump of putrid fat, just a pale ridge

of ropy skin. *¡Perfecto!* A perfect graft.
After fifty years, even the scar has disappeared.

Auras . . .? New Age crystals . . .? Faith healers . . .?
¿Quién sabe . . .? But *¡curanderos . . .!*

I'd almost forgotten my *tlacuache* transplant.

Earthen Vessels

At Frijoles Canyon Visitors' Center,
socially distanced from two sunburnt tourists
—everyone masked—I read a park placard.

Facts, dates, historical context. Drawings
of competent people busy at daily tasks
in thriving fifteenth-century Tyuonyi Pueblo.

Small game carried in yucca baskets, large kills
slung on poles, successful hunters march home.
Masons mix mortar, raise walls. Women tend

gardens, grind maize on stone *metates,* roll
snake-like coils to build narrow-necked water jars,
broad-shouldered seed pots, full-bellied *ollas* for cooking

posole, squash, *frijoles pintos*—speckled beans
grown beside the creek. Tempered by fire,
each pot preserves its maker's fingerprints.

I scoop iron-rich soil into cupped palms. Bold graphics
on my neighbor's shirt: a handmade bowl, captioned
by flowing calligraphy: *Earthen Vessel.*

Excuse me, are you a potter?
I hold up my red clay nuggets. *For forty years
I earned my living making earthen vessels.*

Lips pursed, nostrils flared, she shakes
her head. *This teeshirt came
from a Baptist Women's church retreat.*

Her husband mimes an embrace—velvet-voiced
baritone, born for the spotlight, the pulpit—
We are but earthen vessels in God's hands!

I pocket my fistful of sun-baked clay, grace them
with my brightest tour-guide's smile.
Have a blessèd day!

Paul Robeson Teaches Me to Fly

In the synagogue's overheated basement
    my father hoists me onto his shoulders,

elbows a path toward the stage
    where a storybook giant sings

about a river—a motherless child—
    someone named Joe Hill—a Yiddish lullaby.

Rumbling voice, as deep as that ol' man river
    —when mountains sing, they sound like him.

Daddy pushes me forward:
    She's only five, but she can read.

The Giant leans down, clasps my middle,
    raises me high overheard.

Kite on an updraft, I ride his warm breath,
    soar above upturned faces.

Chest muscles flex, skin prickles.
    Can a little girl grow feathers? Learn to fly?

Sparked by vintage red vinyl 78's,
    memory arcs from axon to dendrite,

rouses dreaming stem-cells
    in bone marrow's dark nursery.

Limbs that once defied gravity never forget.

A Heart Is Not a Valentine

It's a fist-sized clump of muscle,
a pump powered by electricity—
prone to damage, break-down.

At sixteen, in love with Tolstoy's tragic heroines,
I joined a Russian language class—fell hard
for Natalya Borisova, my teacher.

Her name melted on my tongue
—spoonful of tangy gooseberry jam
in a glass of scalding black tea.

My heart sang muted harmonies in her choir,
quavered when Natalya noticed me.
Days later her heart stopped.

Rheumatic fever—twenty-five years old.
Menstrual cramps turned me inside out
when I heard—blood flowed for two weeks.

When I was pregnant two hearts beat
inside my body—I couldn't tell them apart.
When your heart stopped

paramedics shocked it with paddles. Surgeons
pried open your ribcage, installed new plumbing—
like replacing blocked hoses in the engine of a car.

Sleepless, I press my cheek to your chest.
Precise as a second hand on its circuit,
your heartbeat ticks off the time.

A heart is not a valentine.

Proof Positive

Should I get an appointment?
Just wait and see?

Stephanie raises her pendulum—
faceted crystal dangles on a thin black cord.

It swings, spins, stops—points straight down
at my left breast. As if my conscience

had spoken. She claims her pendulum's
solved my dilemma, brushes off my doubts.

Her father was a world-class rocket-scientist.
When three costly eighty-foot shafts

on his land yielded only dry sand,
he hired a dowser. Divining rods flexed

like iron in a blacksmith's forge.
Their new well never ran dry.

Invasive Species

At each new campground tents sprout
overnight like exotic mushrooms.
Fruit-salad colors: watermelon,
mango, lime, tangerine.

Shoehorned into tight spaces, strangers
build invisible walls. Lone campers engage
with their gear, couples orbit each other, wildlife
goes to ground. Alien weeds hitch rides

on knobby hiking boots. Stowaways in backpack
pockets, fast-growing seeds fall to earth,
take root and thrive. Developers eye reserves.
Even mindful travelers alter the landscape.

At Lake Ohau a through-hiker shucks off
her forty-liter pack, makes camp facing
the shore. Arianwen—from Oz—
walks beside me to the toilets.

Inside, a mewling bundle of calico fur
snakes around our ankles.
Does this amber-eyed charmer
subsist on hand-outs?

Runaway rabbits infest Aotearoa,
but flightless kiwi birds
make easier prey. From a wall-poster
I read names of foreign invaders run amok,

native flora & fauna displaced
by invasive species.
With a gentle boot,
Arianwen pushes the kitten away.

If English Nouns Had Gender

would you pump raw sewage
into a virgin river? Use a copper-colored
slot canyon as a garbage dump?

In English, landscape's just real estate—
an "it" for us to exploit. When we destroy it,
is our language to blame for our indifference?

I've always wondered, does language shape
a people's worldview, or do people shape
language to reflect their view of the world?

Is grammar the chicken or the egg?
Would our behavior change
if English nouns had gender?

La montaña—feminine. That never stopped
Spanish-speakers from dynamiting
her flanks, plundering *her* silver, *her* gold.

L'arbre—masculine. When Frenchmen need firewood
they don't ask *his* permission, beg *his* forgiveness
—they chop *him* down, strike the match.

Like most immigrants' children, I shuttled
back and forth on a bridge of words,
translating for uneasy neighbors.

English: muscular, action-packed—anchored
in the Here & Now—hard-headed
Master of Practical Things.

Spanish: sings from the heart—rings
like church bells—throbs like flamenco guitars.
Distinguishes between what is and what might be.

My two languages—different keys
to crack life's secret code. I need both
—they've made me who I am.

My Husband's Pacemaker

Wobbly as a beat-up bicycle wheel (flat tire, warped rim,
broken spokes), my husband's heart faltered.

Worn-out wiring sputtered. Oxygen-starved muscles
howled like wolf-cubs cut off from their pack.

But now, driven by his state-of-the-art electronic pacemaker,
atria and ventricles pump in synch, deliver a steady beat.

Before falling asleep he considers the what-ifs—
what if this gadget quits working? . . . what if I don't wake up?

Wounded flesh still healing over his high-tech device,
his heart thumps under my hand. I picture

tiny comic-book lightning bolts zapping faulty circuits
in blood-filled chamber walls.

Will died once before. EMTs cut off his club jersey,
fired three high-voltage charges into his chest.

After open-heart surgery he confirmed our expectations:
no blinding light, golden harps, welcome-committee

of silver-winged kin-folk waiting at the gate
with outstretched arms. I weigh our choices:

A—To be buried, become food
for tunneling earthworms, burgeoning roots.

B—Consign our bodies to the fire,
our ashes to the wind.

Daily rituals sustain us: make the tea, set the table,
watch the news, wash the dishes. Before I decide

what to cook for dinner, I always offer him choices.
Perhaps I should ask Will now which he'd prefer.

Pueblo Bonito's Ghosts

shadow me through roofless rooms
that stare at the sun like lidless eyes.
I try to picture family life in this multi-storied

masterpiece—three centuries' labor
abandoned in haste, before masons laid
the first cornerstone for Notre Dame's cathedral.

My fingers trace stonework as varied
as medieval tapestries, every panel
embroidered by a different pair of hands.

Did masons compete to create the most pleasing
designs? A Park Ranger says walls were plastered
with adobe, each room decorated by its occupant.

Did five-year-olds scribble on bedroom walls? Did parents
record growing children's heights beside doorways?
The Ranger points to a stone-age kitchen appliance—

a metate—for grinding corn to make tortillas.
He asks, *Do you know what this is?* I tell him I grew up
eating corn tortillas, but struggled to make them.

I mime clapping motions to flatten *bolitas de maza*
with uneven hands—right ring-finger and pinkie
curled tight like cocktail shrimp. The Ranger chuckles.

Ear pressed against stone warm as skin
I hear—nothing. Pueblo Bonito's ghosts
have left me to fill in the gaps.

20 Pages, 100 Questions

Application for Naturalization

In Cuidad Juarez pretty girls are prey.
Twenty-five years ago Alma fled north.
Volunteer tutor, I help her fill in the blanks.

> *Have you ever been a habitual drunkard?* _____
>
> *Have you ever committed a crime,*
> *served a prison sentence?* _____
>
> *Engaged in, or compelled someone else to engage in*
> *Prostitution?* _____ *Armed insurrection?* _____
>
> *Are you a Nazi? Communist? Terrorist?* _____

(When my teenaged Russian-Jewish father
reached Ellis Island, did the gate-keeper ask,
*Are you an Anarchist? Socialist? Bolshevist?*_____)

I drill Alma for the final hurdle—her in-person interview
with *la Migra,* daunting as Class V rapids—
boulders, whirlpools, thundering chutes.

> *Applicant must demonstrate English proficiency,*
> *knowledge of US History and Government.*

The 20-page study guide—blue, like my American passport
—contains 100 questions. How many home-grown patriots
could pass this exam? I quiz Alma on Zoom,

frown when she slips into Spanish. On bus rides—
—lunch breaks—late nights at her kitchen table—
she squints at her blue booklet's small print.

Sprawled beside the TV like seals on a sun-warmed rock,
her US-born teenagers nudge each other, mimic the way
Mamá cracks her knuckles, how she gnaws her lower lip.

Part 3:
Stress Fractures

How We Were Raised

If you want to be safe, be invisible—
curbside sparrow on a crowded street,

translucent minnow
in a rushing stream.

That's how we were raised. Clothing
should camouflage, designed to conceal.

> *On your way home, lower your eyes.*
> *If you hear catcalls, walk faster.*
>
> *Remember, men are wolves,*
> *you're the rabbit.*
>
> *If you must go out alone,*
> *be home before dark.*

Rules learned in childhood,
long forgotten—till a stranger

raises his walking stick, swings at me
—hawk-eyed slugger aiming

for the outfield. I careen left,
bolt past him, glance back.

Hand on his crotch, he cackles, shouts,
> *Next time around, I'll nail you!*

I quicken my stride. His unhinged laughter
clings like dog-shit on a hiking shoe.

I remember now, how it feels
to be the rabbit.

Grace's Broken Statue

(for my mother)

As I rub lemon oil into smooth wood
memories rise like flotsam at high tide.
Mommy hefts a mahogany block

as long and slim as her arm, rummages
her tomato-red toolbox—grinning maw
with files, awls, knives, for teeth.

Fidgety five-year-old, I am denied entry
to my mother's magic realm.
No snack, no bedtime story.

I won't call her "Mommy" anymore.
Chisel in hand, Grace sits rapt.
Cat-like vocal cords thrum.

Hungry swallows, her hands
swoop and dart. Honed steel
bites into red-brown wood,

curlicue shavings fall, wood-chips fly.
Ruthless, Grace carves away everything
extra—corners succumb, curves swell.

I'm watching a hatchling emerge
from its shell. Flushed with goddess-power,
she makes the dead branch dance,

gives pure form a pulse. Lovestruck,
Grace polishes the slender legs
of the woman she's just birthed.

Decades later my mother gifts me
her long-limbed lady—broken feet
glued on—scrapes, gouges

disguised by skillful sanding.
In one of her frequent Van Gogh moods
she'd flung her delicate statue two stories down.

When I grimace, Grace bristles.
I like her better this way, my mother says.
Now she tells the truth.

The Performer

He yanked out lashes till his eyelids were bare.
Gnawed at his nails—raw fingertips bled.
I noticed, but never understood.

Fox caught in a foot-trap, he was poised to chew off
his mutilated paw. Disguised in the frilly clothes
his mother chose, he played the part, took pains

to avoid behavior that might upset doting parents,
unsuspecting siblings, stiff-necked Father Beecham
who'd baptized him, naive neighbors like me.

Trained to please, to entertain, he did cartwheels,
danced on tightropes, rode a unicycle, balanced
spinning porcelain plates on poles, juggled

flaming torches. For his big sister's wedding
his mother made up his face, brushed and sprayed
his glossy blond hair, dressed him in petal-soft silk.

Behind a flurry of white-gloved hands, bridesmaids agreed
—hazel-eyed beauty with a *Vogue* model's shape,
the shy Maid of Honor rivaled the bride.

At the reception he waltzed with his father.
Next morning a few of his brother's clothes,
his backpack and bike were gone.

His mother told me she'd found the clippers
beside the bathroom sink. Hope's glossy hair
was stuffed in the wastebasket underneath.

Needlework

My knuckles bent on demand—
once steady hands coaxed the finest thread

through the needle's eye. But even then,
I never enjoyed sewing.

Mother taught me to repair seams, replace
buttons, patch worn-out elbows, torn knees.

No need now for hand-me-downs
—but poverty's habits die hard.

Driven out by vodka-fueled Cossacks
fierce as packs of hyenas, my relatives

sewed documents, coins, wedding rings
inside coat linings. Hardship built heritage.

In Pennsylvania's oil patch, my husband's
Welsh grandmother stitched wedding quilts

—one for each bride, small quilts for cradles. Will slept
under the quilt that warmed older cousins, two sisters,

then our daughter, two grandsons. When swaddled
in rainbows and skilled needlework, are dreams sweeter?

After finding a three-inch rip in his pocket,
Will discards serviceable pants. During evening news,

I fetch Mother's sewing kit. Needlework buffers images
from Ukraine—blackened rubble, burnt-out cars,

bodies strewn like rag dolls on railway platforms.
I make tiny stitches, evenly spaced, pull the thread tight.

Nuclear Triptych

1—The Hill

Four times a year my husband and I drive ninety miles
to sell our handmade pottery on The Hill. Peace signs
and political slogans adorn our van's rear bumper.

The Hill, aka Los Alamos—doomsday's armory, cradle
of Little Boy and Fat Man. "Top Secret" in 1943,
now a thriving colony of PhD's and millionaires.

With nowhere to spend generous pay cheques
and little to do while brown hands sweep floors,
wash clothes, change diapers, cook dinner,

sophisticated spouses of nuclear physicists and engineers
welcome artists at festivals—outside Fuller Lodge
in warm weather, inside the high school gym when it snows.

They buy our paintings, pottery, jewelry, handwoven
shawls; greet us as old friends. Yet we are outsiders,
like labor bussed in from Taos, Española,

Tesuque, Santa Clara Pueblo. My children
went to college on money we made
selling our pottery on The Hill.

Unlike Navajo uranium miners,
Hispanic construction crews, janitors,
maintenance men, drives of excavators

who bury radioactive waste, my family
paid no price for our nation to become
"Death, the Destroyer of Worlds."

Four times a year we drive ninety miles
to sell our pottery on the Hill. Peace signs
and political slogans adorn our van's rear bumper.

2—Ground Zero

On this gusty February day, clouds like greasy soap suds
smother the sky. At the electrified gate an officer barks:
    DO NOT leave the paved road!
        (Unexploded ordinance . . .) DO NOT stop! DO NOT touch
           anything! DO NOT pocket even a pebble.
        (Radioactive . . .)

On heavily guarded White Sands Missile Range,
our peloton of recreational cyclists trails
a squat army jeep across a cratered moonscape.
    In 1945, if "The Gadget" had gone wrong,
    would our green planet now look like this?

Ground Zero's scorched eye-socket—half a mile wide
—glares as we pose beside the black obelisk.
Its bronze plaque states facts, not Why's or What-if's.
    No splinters remain of the jade-green Trinitite
        once prized for earrings, necklaces, paperweights.

After the last question, the final snapshot, we remount
our bikes, follow the jeep to the gate. Along northbound I-25,
between the Trinity Site and The Hill where the bomb
    was born, exit signs point to crumbling villages,
    home to 150,000 subsistence farmers in the '40s.

Days after the blast soldiers arrived in Corona
with Geiger counters to measure radioactivity
house to house. Residents refused to let them in.
    You won't find any here, an old rancher grumbled.
    We don't own a radio.

3—Downwinders

Ash blanketed rooftops, blighted gardens, burned
hair off the hides of grazing cows, poisoned cisterns.
Children caught radioactive ash on their tongues,

rubbed it all over their brown skins, joked about Christmas
in July. Graveyards in nearby towns bristle with crosses
like raised porcupine quills.

On my public TV station a Tularosa native tells how
her great-grandmother saw the sun rise in the West, knelt
to pray the Rosary in Spanish as the pre-dawn sky blazed.

She tallies losses—Great-grandmother, Grandfather, Mother,
her own thyroid cancer, her twenty-three-year-old daughter
just diagnosed with thyroid cancer—graduate school on hold.

I wonder if she knew my friend Jan, Tularosa potter
who raised organic vegetables for her family,
made jam with succulent figs from her tree—

all grown with municipal water the whole town drank.
Dead at fifty of brain cancer. Testicular cancer
sickened her twenty-two-year-old son.

My family was never exposed, but my son survived
a rare blood cancer—radiation scars on his heart, his lungs.
I saw him curled on the floor, sweating, shivering, retching.

While I squint at a complex knitting project, the mother
from Tularosa speaks of New Mexico's downwinders—
invisible to nuclear scientists and engineers on The Hill.

Four times a year we drive to Los Alamos
to sell our handmade pottery. Political slogans
and peace signs adorn our van's rear bumper.

Ghost Town

Our tour begins in the shade of Pueblo Bonito. The ranger
gestures toward ghost-filled kivas, grief-stricken walls.

*. . . took four centuries to build Chaco's Great Houses.
Some stood four stories high. Aligned*

*on a North-South axis to track the sun's passage
—Equinox at high noon, full midwinter moon—*

*towering star charts in stone to mark the Center
of Time. Abandoned after a fifty-year drought.*

He leads his gaggle of gray-haired history buffs,
New Age seekers, a tripod-toting photographer

into sky-breached rooms, doorways
even I must stoop to pass through.

Today Chaco's high-rises house lizards, scorpions,
centipedes, mice. Dappled to match shadows and dirt,

a rattlesnake dozes on a roofless kiva's rim.
Aloft, hawks and ravens eye them all.

Fluent in the syntax of clay and adobe, my fingertips
read poems in the Braille of broken stones.

Sleepless at midnight, I'm haunted
by Chaco's astronomer-builders.

My growth-crazed city spawns new suburbs
along our dying river, drains our dwindling aquifer.

In wind-blown *arroyos,* pot shards poke
through parched sand. Indoors, electronic devices

stream neon colors, catchy music, gripping dramas
to keep nagging ghosts at bay.

Starting from Scratch

Once driven by need, now I go thrifting for sport.
In Women's Clothing I sort through pre-owned blouses;
survey skillets, bowls, kitchen utensils in Housewares.

The woman beside me fingers wooden spoons,
mismatched cutlery, a wire whisk; lifts a mixing bowl,
sets it down, hefts chunky white restaurant mugs.

While she tallies prices, counts cash, her son reads
"The Adventures of Curious George" to his sisters.
Matching pink dresses—lace collars and cuffs, bows

tied behind like butterflies' wings—the twins preen
in their mother's handiwork. Brother's white shirt, buttoned
up to his chin. Bluejeans pressed with a crease.

Do they live in an apartment, a trailer? Does she have
steady work, decent pay? I recall starting from scratch
in an unfamiliar country, creating a home

for my small son from other people's leavings.
Brother's finger scrolls down the page. Lips pursed,
noses crinkled, the girls sound out English words.

He frowns. *¡Atención, niñas! En inglés se dice así* . . .
Mother gives up a saucepan, agrees to one book—
¡No más uno!—quells dissent with an eyebrow.

Brother returns three books to the shelf.
Shoulders squared, Mother guides her children
past oblique glances toward the checkout stand,

shadowed by a Thrift-Mart employee.
In line, a beet-faced shopper carps
about *those people* . . .

The Language Barrier

A fortress in conquered territory,
the language barrier keeps us out.

In ESL we recite—numbers, colors, the alphabet.
Name—seasons, months, days of the week.
Memorize, practice, repeat—

phone number, street address.
Name of school or employer.
Country & date of birth.

Twenty-four pairs of nervous lips strain
to break old habits, force stubborn tongues
to take new shapes, copy the way *gringos* talk.

We learn common phrases but still sound
the same—rumbling R's we'll never tame,
vowels we learned by second grade:

A, E, I, O, U, ¡El burro sabe más que tú!
Music our mouths know how to make, beat of *danzón*
and *merengue*—familiar rhythms our ears can follow.

Comfortable with accents thicker than Mexican *crema,*
as spicy as the *salsa cruda* we eat at home,
classmates understand one another.

When I speak to my supervisor at work, clerks
at markets, teachers at my daughter's school,
crooked lines crease white foreheads.

I repeat myself slowly, use my hands, pause to find
the right words. When they raise their voices,
I swallow mine, do my job, follow the rules.

A fortress in conquered territory,
the language barrier keeps us out.

Blind Spots

Flight #2673 filled, except the four facing front seats.
At the window a tall man in a crisply pressed suit
reads the Wall Street Journal.

I claim the seat beside him. Opposite him
the flight attendant straps a young woman down—
small as an eight-year-old, name-tag pinned to her dress.

Shapely legs dangle, patent leather
Mary-Janes crowd his long shins.
Cradling her American Girl doll, she coos,

I love Black people—you have such beautiful skin!
He stiffens—our linked seats recoil.
I cringe—will she try to touch him?

Do you have children? He raises his newspaper
like a shield. *I'm twenty-one, but I'll never have children
because of my size . . . only my doll, Julie.*

She fills our two-hour flight with non-stop chatter.
I notice her fingers—not pudgy, no dimples—
clear polish on neatly trimmed nails.

After landing the flight attendant unbuckles her, takes
her hand. Beloved doll clutched tight, knees brushing
our neighbor's trousers, she croons, *I'll never forget you . . .*

Two decades later I still recall her flutey voice,
his spine-chilling silence. Last week she reappeared
when I called a female doctor "Nurse."

Yesterday she stopped me when I was tempted
to praise the wilderness of tight little braids
in a stranger's amazing waist-length hair.

Routine Screening

Clumsy as river dories, plastic tubs ferry
my backpack, laptop, Kindle and purse
downstream to the X-ray machine.

A female TSA agent pulls me from the Seniors' queue.
You've been randomly selected.
Don't worry darlin'—it's just routine.

Behind radiation-proof glass
a burly officer booms, *Arms overhead,*
like in the picture! Feet, Ma'm!

Painted footprints—crime-scene yellow
—stance too wide for my five-foot frame.
Splayed like a spatchcocked chicken

I hold my breath. The scanner spins—spider
wrapping paralyzed prey. When I step out
the female agent backs me against a wall,

poses me like da Vinci's Vitruvian Man.
Blue nitrile gloves probe my back, armpits,
breasts, ribcage. Squeeze each thigh,

graze my groin, encircle my ankles,
climb to my waist. *Remove your belt.*
Don't worry darlin'. . . it's just routine.

Blue fingers raise my blouse, slither
under my waistband, swab my palms.
I need your shoes for the X-ray machine.

Eyes averted, passengers bolt past me,
jostle beside the conveyer belt.
Will I miss my flight, my grandson's graduation?

When my crocs reappear, the agent chirps,
OK, darlin'—you can go. Jaws clenched,
hands shaking, I collect my belongings.

Shrinking

Why must everyone mumble?
I read lips, but peering at a soft-talker

across a cave-dark room, his mouth
concealed by a jungle of facial hair . . .

I feel like a doomed glacier—shrinking.
My husband tosses his stained shirt to the floor.

I glance at him in the bathroom mirror, remind him,
You aren't alone, as I pluck gray hairs

from my comb. I shed like a Persian cat.
Bones as brittle as yesterday's toast.

I've shrunk three inches in height,
lost core-strength, grip-strength, memory.

Not just names—even simple words,
common phrases. Has my brain gone soft

like some worn-out bicycle tire?
Ten years from now, will I recognize

my own children, recall where I came from?
If you call my name, will I look up?

For decades I made hand-thrown pottery,
pressed my fingerprints onto vases, teapots, mugs.

Fired to white heat, my pots emerged from the flames
dressed in colors of sun-baked canyons, moon-lit lakes.

Historic artifacts, our pottery outlasts us.
Now I work at my keyboard—archeologist

on a dig into my buried past.
My future . . .?

While Fractures and Abrasions Heal

ribs ache, lungs stutter, scraped elbows and knees sting
—as if I've been trampled by runaway mustangs.
I wage war against PTSD, but call for a truce
with pain, the body's wordless language.

Like my lionhearted Siamese cat,
I compensate. In her eighteenth year
Cleo went blind. Long whiskers
as keen as naked nerve-endings

skimmed walls, gauged distances,
sensed directions. She'd climb eight steps,
turn right, climb the final five. Velvet paws
never hesitated—Cleo could count.

If my battered right knee won't tolerate
long hikes anymore, if my wrenched ankle
can't crank my bike's pedals without complaint,
if fear nails my feet to the floor, who will I be?

In the cosmic scale's balance pans
I weigh grit against delusion,
bravado against common sense,
pigheadedness against perseverance.

When Mother's essential tremor—inherited
along with her artist's hands—derailed my career,
I reinvented myself. Am I on the cusp of a different life
—or at the unmarked door of Death's waiting-room?

Epitaph

Weeks after wildfires blackened cottonwoods and tamarisks
along the Rio Grande's drought-starved banks,

the stench lingers. I stroll across puckered sand—
signature of our once mighty river, now sucked dry.

In September I greet the Equinox among Chaco Canyon's
ruins, built centuries ago when more rain fell, water flowed

year-round. Sky-drowned Great Houses, kivas
like empty eye sockets, blind but brimming with light

—a civilization's epitaph written in grieving stone:
slow death by changing climate; sudden death by rockfalls

from cliffs that calve like glaciers. Boulders as tall
as my two-story house, crumbly as timeworn adobe,

weep coarse grit under my hands. Dead cottonwoods
cleave to the arroyo's wasted banks.

Intricate as Chinese calligraphy on a frayed silk scroll,
ink-black twigs depict decades of failed monsoons.

I crane my neck to read clouds overhead, kneel
to trace tide-pools engraved on clifftops—fingerprints

of the ancient Cretaceous Inland Sea. Embedded in limestone
I find fossilized sharks' teeth, a shrimp's silhouette,

the sacred spiral of a nautilus shell. Undimmed by manmade light,
the Milky Way shimmers against midnight's true-black sky.

At home electricity lights my sleepless nights, cooks my meals,
heats my bathwater, powers the keyboard that types

my epitaph for our time of changing climate.
Chaco Canyon's silent ghosts abide.

Part 4:
Knit Together

Wheelchair-Guy at the Sidewalk Cafe

Sunday mornings, a gaggle of spandex-clad cyclists
crowds around a small table, blocks the sidewalk.
Wheelchair-guy faces off against them.

He's child-sized, feisty as a feral cat,
toothpick-legs encased in steel braces,
grizzled stubble like speckled feathers,

owl-eyes magnified by drug-store glasses.
Chairs scrape, kindly mutterings belie
shudders among the able-bodied.

Midweek, sipping coffee alone at the same table, I see him
eyeball a path between my backpack and the curb's edge.
I make eye contact, ask his name, offer mine.

*Do you live nearby? I've watched you navigate
between tables and chairs, splayed knees,
oversized feet.* I point to my neon-orange bike,

I'm scared to ride through tight spaces.
Victor pivots, scoots toward my table, shows off
his high-tech chair's maneuvers. It can spin, lunge

forward and back, zip across busy intersections.
I got street-smarts, Victor brags. *Gotta dodge
stray dogs, pissed-off drivers.*

I raise my old-lady arm, pump a fist.
His laughter crackles like popcorn in a hot pan.
Small talk worn thin, coffee drained, Victor leaves

his take-out cup behind. Stifled questions—
an itch I mustn't scratch. We're not strangers
anymore—we know each other's names.

Among Kin

On the rim of Chetro Ketl's Great Kiva
—an underground cathedral—

I discover a trove of pot shards
arranged by a keen-eyed tourist—

some plain, some embellished
with symbols and patterns applied

with a yucca brush dipped in a brew
of beeweed and crushed iron-rich rock.

In my upturned palm, a concave fragment fits
—as if its maker and I clasped hands.

My fingers remember how wet clay feels,
the way it yields to a knowing touch.

I turn the shard over, discover texture
left by a woven basket—womb

that cradled the growing bowl
while the potter shaped her soft clay.

I want to ask her if she'd been happy,
whether her children were safe, why her people

left home. Would she mind if I took her shard,
resettled it beside pots I've made?

I recall my own migration,
leave the shard among kin.

Showing Up

6:00 AM. NPR News. Hit Parade of Disasters:
*War Crimes in Ukraine, in Gaza, Record-breaking Droughts,
Wildfires Spreading, Glaciers Melting, Sea Levels Rising.*

8:45 AM. We drive past Washington Mid-school: flowers, candles,
handmade cards for the 9th grader murdered by his classmate
during recess. Patricia asks, *What can we do?* I shrug, *Show up?*

9:00 AM. Vacant lot behind our neighborhood community center:
three battered pickups pull in, unload shovels, rakes, saws,
long handled clippers—blades like crabs' claws.

9:15 AM. Volunteers distribute work-gloves, trash bags.
In the gutter snow-melt trickles. Hats, masks come off.
Not gloves! Broken glass, saw-toothed cans, discarded needles . . .

10:00 AM. Under tangled weeds I unearth a spiral notebook,
smashed bifocals, rusty barbed-wire. We stomp on styrofoam
takeout boxes, scraps of crumbling drywall. Scoop, bag, heave . . .

12:00 NOON. Sagging pickup trucks head to the landfill.
Tools safely locked in the janitor's shed,
new friends exchange cellphone numbers.

1:30 PM. Over coffee at Java Junction,
Patricia outlines plans for the community garden.
Will enough volunteers show up?

6:00 PM. I reheat yesterday's green chile stew,
brew a fresh pot of oolong tea,
mute the evening news.

Knit Together

My metal plate still warns me when the weather's
about to change. My faded scar recalls why it's there—
four-inch-long zipper, tiny white stitch marks for teeth.

After the crash my left arm zigzagged
—disconcerting as a sandhill crane's leg,
knobby knee bent backwards.

Dr. Rubinstein rejoined radius and ulna,
screwed a titanium brace across splintered ends.
Eight weeks in a cast, four more in physical therapy.

Given time, outraged bones knit together.
So long as stubborn pulse persists, greedy lungs gulp
oxygen and restless neurons relay vital information,

muscle and bone want to heal, the body's intricate systems
want to work. Surgeons fuse fractured bones, staple
gashed flesh, suture sliced nerves, graft new skin

onto burnt limbs. They bypass clogged arteries,
transplant kidneys, livers, hearts. Could specialists
transfuse hope into countries hemorrhaging

from bone-deep wounds of tribal hate?
Would war-wrecked nations knit together,
given time?

State Road #57

A dotted line on the map between Crown Point
and Chaco Canyon, State Road #57 bisects
a crazy-quilt—Navajo land, federal land, private land.

Hands clamped to the steering wheel, my husband
negotiates hubcap-deep ruts, limestone slabs
like giant stairs, sun-bleached mesas stippled

with cholla cacti, wind-lashed creosote shrubs.
No oncoming cars, power lines, cellphone towers.
No drilling rigs—iron roosters pecking

at barren ground. No road signs. Blinding glare
ahead, billowing dust behind. Propelled
by 21st-century hubris, boasting

computerized traction control and satellite navigation,
our four-wheel drive pickup humps along,
single-minded as a foraging *pinacate* beetle.

Avid readers of the desert's unwritten language,
ancient pilgrims followed stars, made fire, found water,
caught what paltry game this arid land provides.

Priests in womb-dark kivas called them
to celebrate Equinox and Solstice, when sunrise
cleaves the spiral carved atop Fajada Butte.

In teeming plazas they came to feast, dance, trade.
Cacao, macaw feathers, yucca sandals, painted pottery,
precious coral and turquoise changed hands.

Ghosts call me to honor what remains.
Halfway in, the pencil-straight road veers
—needle to an unseen magnet.

When the butte's square head breaks the horizon,
it's as if the Sun Dagger's guardian
reached out to guide my way.

Human Remains

Red lid secured with Scotch tape,
the Tupperware container rests in my lap.

Five years now, since my sister died.
Weeks later my niece found a cardboard box labeled

"Human Remains" on her doorstep. While she drives,
I search the neighborhood for traces of her mother.

A trampoline, a motor-home, an overturned
tricycle in a driveway—everything's in focus

except my sister's face. Road noise deadens
the echoes of her laughter. *Before you were born,*

I tell my niece, *your mother loved to dance.*
Striped skirt spinning like Saturn's rings,

long hair airborne like soaring wings,
eyes shut, arms reaching . . . for what?

What did she see through the ruby-red screen
of closed lids? Plum-purple bruises

under her dress? Were killer addictions—
alcohol, sex, cocaine—written into her DNA?

Nobody named the family demons.
Did music's magic fail her? Did I?

Just before sundown we reach the shore.
Gauzy clouds, lilac and rose, blur the line

where sea meets sky. Gulls wheel overhead.
My niece asks me to speak. I choke, whisper,

I miss you. She peels back the lid, spills
something gray and gritty as beach sand—

a small mound, dissolved by an outgoing wave.

What Our Bodies Know

I wear my feelings on my face. You rein yours in.
Laser-focused, you lash out when I distract you.

Multitasker on overdrive, I bristle when you bellow,
SLOW DOWN! WHY CAN'T YOU JUST LISTEN?

Tectonic plates, we grind against each other.
Small tremors escalate, bedrock buckles, shifts.

A Grand Canyon-sized rift
yawns between us.

Sparks fly over trivia—your remarks
about how I wash dishes, my full-throated

profanity when I trip on your muddy boots.
Words bruise. Sarcasm bites. Eyes narrowed,

you snarl, *WHY CAN'T YOU JUST BE NICE?*
I seethe, jaws clenched, blood pressure climbing.

Small cuts fester, leave scars. Old grievances
—shrapnel lodged deep in bone.

Ancient nag with a broken leg
—numb, useless, mind in a fog—

I limp from stove to sink, my refuge
now a bog of curdled milk, rancid butter.

Bed in a muddle, we lash out at ghosts, grapple
with sweaty sheets. Open windows beg for breeze.

Lords of the predawn hush,
coyotes sing to their mates.

Jackhammer pulse—your arms clasped
around mine—my hand curled inside yours.

A Visitation

April morning, yellow and blue. Cotton-ball clouds.
Insects' thrum. Dew-drenched leaves sparkle
like glass shards. Sudden clatter, frenzied blur—

a great blue heron, my favorite bird, explodes
through dense foliage. I freeze, squint,
shade my eyes. Sky-hungry wings climb.

Iceberg-blue, snake-necked, rapier-beaked,
laser-eyed impaler of fish and small rodents,
trailing legs like stalks of bamboo;

T-Rex's unlikely descendant, Pharaoh's original Phoenix;
among First Americans, messenger from the gods.
Smitten with their fluid lines and mystical ties,

I've drawn hundreds of herons on my freshly-thrown pots.
Wading—in flight—stalking prey in eddies—
weightless ballet dancers poised on one slender leg.

My herons too endured fire, emerged from the kiln
cloaked in colors of iron, cobalt, copper—minerals born
in the planet's molten core, mined from its jagged crust.

Solitary migrant—lineage inscribed in the fossil record
soon after sea-creatures traded fins for wings—
graceful demigod painted inside Egyptian tombs.

Tell me, can you see through Time?
Have you brought me messages?
Nameless, mute, my ancestors never visit.

The heron circles, dips, soars, flies off—but not too far—
disappears into the canopy. Then reappears . . . twice more . . .
Steadfast, she leads me on, lures me away from her nest.

Old People

My husband's aunts & uncles always vacationed together.
A flock of frosty-feathered snow-birds, each winter
they landed in my mother-in-law's Florida mobile home.

While they discussed beta-blockers, bypass surgeries,
diabetic neuropathy, I fussed over my six-year-old son's
bruised knees, fretted about my infant daughter's colic.

Eyes cataract-clouded, claws arthritic, dowagers' humps,
leathery skin wrinkled like an elephant's hide—I saw
those old people as members of a different tribe.

Today my son needs reading glasses. Like his father,
he's hard of hearing. We fly across five states
to visit our daughter, cheer from the bleachers

for grandsons at varsity track meets, intramural soccer games.
I wonder, how do they see us? In the minefield of our eighties
we tiptoe past unexploded ordinance.

My husband's pacemaker rides piggyback, keeps his pulse
on track. Grateful for titanium knees, new hips—cobalt-chromium,
ceramic, polyethylene—old friends relearn how to walk.

I mind my feet as I climb to my upstairs bedroom, wary
of fracturing another osteoporotic bone. An age-spot
darkens my forehead. Deeply etched wrinkles

crosshatch my cheeks. While I comb thinning gray hair,
half-forgotten faces appear in my bathroom mirror. A flock
of frosty-feathered snow-birds closes ranks around me.

The Food Chain

White fluff drifts midair. A mound of goose-down at my feet
—enough to fill two king-sized pillows and a comforter.

Fierce fighters, six-foot wingspans. No lone coyote
could take down a full-grown goose, eat the carcass whole.

I knew the pair of Canadas that nested here. Vigilant parents,
they nudged their brood of seven fuzz balls, winnowed to four

half-fledged goslings—into the water when I came too near.
The killers left no scraps—flensed thigh bone, iron beak,

scaly leg, leathery foot armed with grappling hooks.
Only this billowing mound—a tattered wedding gown

dumped on the ground. In time south winds shredded it,
left gauzy scraps snagged on brown grass; uncovered

a gray wingtip, flight feathers splayed like frantic fingers,
purple bloodstains, blackened bits of sunbaked flesh.

Decades ago I became vegetarian, but I recall
how pregnancy turned me into a voracious carnivore,

how I claimed my place at the top of the food chain, taught
my babies to grasp a juicy chicken leg with tiny fingers,

gnaw tender meat with new front teeth. I picture a litter
of suckling coyote pups—eyes glued shut, pink bellies plump,

gooseflesh morphing into rich milk,
quill and claw into silky fur, prey into predator.

When I pass this place on my daily walk
I'll think of a wedding gown dumped on the ground.

Elegy for Our Garden

Midday sun—glass blower's glory hole.
Afternoon wind—dust-devil's playground.
Fifty-year drought—river's death sentence.
      High-desert gardening—heartbreaker.

We've lived too long tethered to raised beds,
coaxing stubborn seeds to sprout, pulling weeds,
patching leaky hoses. I'm done battling squash bugs,
      tomato worms thicker than my thumb.

Greedy snow peas, eggplants, arugula
yield little for all the water they guzzle,
devoted care they demand of your creaky back,
      my stiff knuckles, dodgy knee.

Meanwhile the polar vortex slides south, glaciers melt,
keystone species teeter on extinction's edge.
Virgin forests become funeral pyres. Summer
      comes sooner, burns hotter, stays longer.

Last July the once mighty Rio Grande ran dry.
In late March a blizzard swaddled mountaintops.
April's freak heatwave unleashed flash floods
      —*café con leche* runoff—too early, too fast.

Now kayakers glide downstream grinning like Huck Finn,
salute me with raised paddles. Beside the bank
a muskrat—mud-brown, plump as a pampered house cat,
      shaggy as a janitor's mop—rides the current,

nose just above water. Rushing stream gurgles,
reeds purr. A pair of snowy egrets wings north.
Generations of nomads stir in my bones.
      I'm done with gardening. Come with me to the river.

Cave People

Inside Sandia Cave's womb-dark hollow
—ceiling blackened by cook-fires
ten thousand years old—I imagine ancestors
crouched elbow to elbow, feeding embers

through frigid nights. When wolf-howls pierce
the blackest hour, do they pray? Bargain with fickle gods?
What bedtime stories do they tell their children
to keep night-terrors at bay?

My fingertips probe a wall as if to feel some trace
of their presence. I try to picture myself
spread-eagled, nose-to-cliff, scurrying crab-wise
toward the noisy creek one hundred feet below.

I would have been a maker of useful things—
yucca baskets, stone tools—spent my days chipping
chunks of quartz into perfectly shaped spearpoints,
knives sharp enough to butcher mastodons.

But could I stay focused,
knowing razor-fanged cats skulked
in overhead branches, giant bears rose
on hind legs to scent human flesh?

My son laments the shambles his son will inherit.
I remind him, cave people's offspring learned to channel
scarce water, farm barren lands, follow heaven's roadmap,
build stone cities with keen minds and callused hands.

Whoever survives this world we've made—
warring tribes, violent weather, fire and flood
—might welcome bedtime stories
about brave people who lived in caves.

Concerto

Refugees from the ordinary, we've dressed
for the occasion. We enter the sanctuary hungry
for magic, for transcendence. Ticket stubs matched

to seat numbers, we squeeze past jutting knees,
juggle coats, handbags, dripping umbrellas
—restless passengers waiting for take-off.

On stage musicians tune their instruments—
nervous cacophony without rhythm or direction.
Lights dim—adrenalin flows. Time to perform.

The soloist steps from the wings,
bows, flips coat tails behind the bench,
sits brooding over the Steinway.

In mandatory black frock coat, white shirt,
loose trousers, sensible shoes, the conductor
takes the podium, bows, pivots, raises her baton.

Piano trickles—ice-bound creek beginning to thaw.
Strings croon, woodwinds swell—birdsong at dawn.
Brass blares, timpani thunders—wild horses stampede.

From the front seats to the balcony's highest row, nerves
vibrate in synch with plucked strings—kindled with longing,
fired by a hundred instruments fused into a single voice.

Recorded, the concerto's a caged menagerie.
Performed live it's a primeval forest—cave bears,
saber-toothed tigers and wooly mammoths run free.

Orchestra and piano explode in a deafening finale.
The baton's last downstroke jolts us to our feet
Throbbing   Triumphant   In love

About the Author

Born to American parents, Johanna DeMay grew up in Mexico City. Like many expatriate children, she shuttled back and forth on a bridge of words, translating for uneasy neighbors. Poetry became her chosen way to knit her worlds together. Encouraged while still in her teens by Pulitzer prize-winning poet and fellow ex-patriot George Oppen, she has never stopped writing.

DeMay became an immigrant again when she resettled in New Mexico with her husband. For forty years the couple earned their living as studio potters while raising two children and building their solar adobe home. Her life took root in clay soil beside the Rio Grande, in a community founded in the mid-18th century by Sephardic refugees on the run from the Inquisition, on land where Native Americans have lived continuously for thousands of years.

She embraces her neighbors, their shared history and traditions, their efforts to build a future together in their beloved place. The high desert taught DeMay to love light, burning blue skies and vast distances. Place shapes her life; place speaks through everything she writes.

Now retired from her ceramics career, DeMay divides her time between writing and volunteering with the immigrant community. She tutors new residents studying to improve their language skills and take their citizenship exams. Many of her poems reflect experiences of displacement and transition—her own as well as those of the people with whom she works.

DeMay honed her craft at workshops taught by luminaries like Marge Piercy, Ellen Bass, Kevin Young, Thomas Lux, Tony Barnstone, Jennifer Clement, and Terese Svoboda, as well as UK Poet Laureates Carol Ann Duffy and Sir Andrew Motion.

Her poems have appeared in three anthologies and in journals such as *I-70 Review, poem, The MacGuffin, Constellations, bosque, Passager, The Main Street Rag, Loch Raven Review, Burningword Literary Journal, Rust and Moth,* and *The Concho River Review.* She has twice received nominations for a Pushcart Prize. Her first full poetry collection, *Waypoints,* was released by Finishing Line Press in 2022.

www.ingramcontent.com/pod-product-compliance
Lightning Source LLC
Chambersburg PA
CBHW030052170426
43197CB00010B/1486